Daily Thoughts of Love

BY GERARD KALAN

SUNSHINE MOUNTAIN PRODUCTIONS, INC.
Derry, New Hampshire

for Lois Hanrahan

Daily Thoughts of Love
©1997, Sunshine Mountain Productions, Inc., 55 Crystal Ave, Suite 248, Derry NH 03038.
All rights reserved.
Cover and page design by Lathrop Design
Printed in Canada

ISBN 1-890017-15-9

January 1

Ah! what is love! It is a pretty thing,
As sweet unto a shepherd as a king.

ROBERT GREENE

January 2

All love at first, like generous wine,
Ferments and frets until 'tis fine.

SAMUEL BUTLER

January 3

Music I heard with you was more than music,
And bread I broke with you was more than bread.

CONRAD AIKEN

January 4

All love is sweet,
Given or returned, Common as light is love,
And its familiar voice wearies not ever.

PERCY BYSSHE SHELLEY

January 5

Love not me for comely grace,
For my pleasing eye or face,
Nor for any outward part,
No, nor for a constant heart.

ANONYMOUS

January 6

Absence from whom we love is worse than death.

WILLIAM COWPER

January 7

In her first passion woman loves her lover,
In all others all she loves is love.

LORD BYRON

January 8

For in my mind, of all mankind, I love but you alone.

ANONYMOUS

January 9

Ah, love, let us be true to one another!

MATTHEW ARNOLD

January 10

All love, all liking, all delight
Lies drown'd with us in endless night.

HESPERIDES

January 11

That Love is all there is,
Is all we know of Love;
It is enough, the freight should be
Proportioned to the groove.

EMILY DICKINSON

January 12

I was in love with loving.

SAINT AUGUSTINE

January 13

The sort of girl I liked to see
Smiles down from her great height at me.

JOHN BETJEMAN

January 14

All for love or the world well lost.

JOHN DRYDAN

January 15

What fond and wayward thoughts will slide
Into a lover's head!

WILLIAM WORDSWORTH

January 16

If all the world and love were young,
And truth in every shepherd's tongue,
These pretty pleasures might me move,
To live with thee and be thy love.

WALTER RALEGH

January 17

I was more true to Love than Love to me.

ANONYMOUS

January 18

All mankind love a lover.

RALPH WALDO EMERSON

January 19

She looked at me as she did love
And made sweet moan
And sure in language strange, she said,
"I love thee true!"

JOHN KEATS

January 20

Where love is great, the littlest doubts are fear:
When little fears grow great, great love grows there.

WILLIAM SHAKESPEARE

January 21

How much better is thy love than wine!

BIBLE, OLD TESTAMENT

January 22

Love seeketh not itself to please,
Nor for itself hath any care,

WILLIAM BLAKE

January 23

Who can give law to lovers? Love is a greater law to itself.

BOETIUS

January 24

And love can come to everyone,
the best things in life are free.

LEW BROWN AND BUDDY DESYLVA

January 25

Breathless, we flung us on the windy hill,
Laughed in the sun, and kissed the lovely grass.

RUPERT BROOKE

January 26

Familiar acts are beautiful through love.

PERCY BYSSHE SHELLEY

January 27

To love or not; in this we stand or fall.

JOHN MILTON

January 28

**Or bid me love ... and I will give
A loving heart to thee.**

ROBERT HERRICK

January 29

How do I love thee? Let me count the ways.

ELIZABETH BARRETT BROWNING

January 30

Oh, my luv is like a red, red rose,
That's newly sprung in June.

ROBERT BURNS

January 31

One of the best things about love is just recognizing a man's step when he climbs the stairs.

COLETTE

February 1

My true love hath my heart, and I have his,
By just exchange one for the other given:
I hold his dear, and mine he cannot miss,
There never was a better bargain driven.

SIR PHILIP SIDNEY

February 2

Every lover is a warrior and Cupid has his camps.

OVID

February 3

Nothing reopens the springs of love so fully as absence,
and no absence so thoroughly as that which must
needs be endless.

ANTHONY TROLLOPE

February 4

Love alone is capable of uniting living beings in such a way
as to complete and fulfill them, for it alone takes them and
joins them by what is deepest in themselves.

PIERRE TEILHARD DE CHARDIN

February 5

The woman is increasingly aware that love alone can give her full stature.

CARL GUSTAV JUNG

February 6

This is my home of love; if I have ranged
Like him that travels, I return again.

WILLIAM SHAKESPEARE

February 7

Out upon it, I have loved
Three whole days together;
And am like to love three more,
If it proves fair weather

SIR. JOHN SUCKLING

February 8

Though love and all its pleasures are but toys,
they shorten tedious nights.

JOHN DAVIES

February 9

Thou shall love and be loved forever; a
Hand like this hand
Shall throw open the gates of new life to thee!

ROBERT BROWNING

February 10

I both love and do not love, and am mad and am not mad.

ANACREON

February 11

Let us not to the marriage of true minds
Admit impediments. Love is not love
Which alters when its alteration finds,
Or bends with the remover to remove.

WILLIAM SHAKESPEARE

February 12

Life is full of opportunities for learning love. … And the one
eternal lesson for all of us is how better we can love.

HENRY DRUMMOND

February 13

I am pleased that you have learned to love a hyacinth. The mere habit of learning to love is the thing.

JANE AUSTEN

February 14

Whoever lives true life will love true love.

ELIZABETH BARRETT BROWNING

February 15

All everything that I understand, I understand only because I love.

LEO TOLSTOY

February 16

Love is fostered by confidence and constancy; he who is able to give much is able also to love much.

SEXTUS PROPERTIUS

February 17

Ideally, both members of a couple in love free each other to new and different worlds.

ANNE MORROW LINDBERGH

February 18

Love looks not with the eye but with the mind.

WILLIAM SHAKESPEARE

February 19

Love is not thinking about it, it is doing it. It is loving.

Eric Butterworth

February 20

The supreme happiness of life is the conviction that we are
loved, loved for ourselves.

Victor Hugo

February 21

Love and gentle heart are one, same thing.

DANTE ALIGHIERI

February 22

**Love consists in this, that two solitudes protect and touch
and greet each other.**

RAINER MARIA RILKE

February 23

Come live with me and be my love,
And we will all the pleasures prove.

CHRISTOPHER MARLOWE

February 24

Love does not consist in gazing at each other, but in looking
outward together in the same direction.

ANTOINE DE SAINT EXUPERY

February 25

Many waters cannot quench love, neither can the floods drown it.

SONG OF SOLOMON

February 26

And still to love, though prest with ill,
In wintry age to feel no chill,
With me is to be lovely still,
My Mary!

WILLIAM COWPER

February 27

Love with delight discourses in my mind
Upon my lady's admirable gifts.

DANTE ALIGHIERI

February 28

I am two fools, I know,
For loving, and for saying so
In whining poetry.

JOHN DONNE

March 1

If love is the answer, could you rephrase the question?

LILY TOMLIN

March 2

In real love, you want the other person's good.
In romantic love, you want the other person.

MARGARET ANDERSON

March 3

And this maiden she lived with no other thought
Than to love and be loved by me.

EDGAR ALLEN POE

March 4

Love is a contagious and virulent disease which leaves a
victim in a state of near imbecility, paralysis, profound
melancholia, and sometimes culminates in death.

QUENTIN CRISP

March 5

My silks and fine array,
My smiles and languished air,
By love are driv'n away;
And mournful lean Despair
Brings me yew to deck my grave:
Such end true lovers have.

WILLIAM BLAKE

March 6

Time, which strengthens friendship, weakens love.

JEAN DE LA BRUYERE

March 7

Beauty soon grows familiar to the lover:
Fades in his eye, and palls upon the sense.

JOSEPH ADDISON

March 8

Twice or thrice had I loved thee,
Before I knew thy face or name.

JOHN DONNE

March 9

A mighty pain to live it is,
And 'tis a pain that pain to miss,
But of all pains, the greatest pain
It is to love, but love in vain.

ABRAHAM COWLEY

March 10

Pains of love be sweeter far
Than all other pleasures are.

JOHN DRYDEN

March 11

So long as man remains free, he strives for nothing so incessantly and so painfully as to find someone to worship.

FYODOR DOSTOYEVSKY

March 12

If love is judged by most of its effects, it resembles hate
more than friendship.

DUC FRANCOIS DE LA ROCHEFOUCAULD

March 13

Love is ridiculous passion which hath no being but in play-books and romances.

JONATHAN SWIFT

March 14

It is impossible to love and to be wise.

FRANCIS BACON

March 15

Love is the child of illusion and the parent of disillusion.

MIGUEL DE UNAMUNO

March 16

From this arises the question whether it is better to be loved rather than feared, or feared rather than loved. It might perhaps be answered that we should wish to be both; but since love and fear can hardly exist together, if we must chose between them, it is far safer to be feared than loved.

NICCOLO MACHIAVELLI

March 17

Love is a springtime plant that perfumes everything with its hope, even the ruins to which it clings.

GUSTAVE FLAUBERT

March 18

Love is a disease which fills you with a desire to be desired.

HENRI DE TOULOUSE-LAUTREC

March 19

Never the time and the place
And the loved one all together!

ROBERT BROWNING

March 20

Friendship is a disinterested commerce between equals; love
an abject intercourse between tyrants and slaves.

OLIVER GOLDSMITH

March 21

When one is in love, one begins by deceiving oneself, one ends by deceiving others. That is what the world calls romance.

OSCAR WILDE

March 22

For though I know he loves me,
Tonight my heart is sad.
His kiss was not so wonderful
As all the dreams I had.

SARA TEASDALE

March 23

One is very crazy when in love.

SIGMUND FREUD

March 24

Love is a gross exaggeration of the difference between one person and everybody else.

GEORGE BERNARD SHAW

March 25

You love me so much you want to put me in your pocket.
And I should die there smothered.

D.H. LAWRENCE

March 26

We declare that love cannot exist between two people who
are married to each other. For lovers give to each other
freely, and under no compulsion; married people are in
duty bound to give into each other's desires.

MARIE COUNTESS OF CHAMPAGNE

March 27

Love is an act of endless forgiveness.

PETER USTINOV

March 28

Love is the answer, but while you are waiting for the answer, sex raises some pretty good questions.

WOODY ALLEN

March 29

Where is the love, beauty and truth we seek,
But in our mind?

PERCY BYSSHE SHELLEY

March 30

Love doesn't grow on the trees like apples in Eden - it's something you have to make. And you must use your imagination to make it too, just like anything else.

JOYCE CAREY

March 31

Romance and work are great diversions to keep you from dealing with yourself.

CHER

April 1

Now I adore my life
With the Bird, the abiding Leaf,
With the Fish, the questing Snail,
And the Eye altering all;
And I dance with William Blake
For love, for Love's sake.

THEODORE ROETHKE

April 2

In Hollywood all marriages are happy. It's trying to live
together afterward that causes all the problems.

SHELLEY WINTERS

April 3

Neither a lofty degree of intelligence, nor imagination, nor
both together go to the making of genius.
Love, love, love, that is the soul of genius.

WOLFGANG AMADEUS MOZART

April 4

I love Mickey Mouse more than any
woman I have ever known.

WALT DISNEY

April 5

What a recreation it is to be in love. It sets the heart aching so delicately, there's no taking a wink of sleep for the pleasure of the pain.

GEORGE COLMAN

April 6

It's curious how when you're in love you yearn to go about doing acts of kindness to everybody.

P.G. WODEHOUSE

April 7

The only difference between a caprice and a life-long passion is that the caprice lasts a little longer.

OSCAR WILDE

April 8

When first we met we did not guess
That Love would prove so hard a master.

ROBERT BRIDGES

April 9

To be in love is merely to be in a state of perceptual anesthesia; to mistake an ordinary young man for a Greek god or an ordinary young woman for a goddess.

H.L. MENCKEN

April 10

Lovers who have nothing to do but love each other are not really to be envied; love and nothing else very soon is nothing else.

WALTER LIPPMANN

April 11

Great loves too must be endured.

COCO CHANEL

April 12

The worst of having a romance is that it leaves one
so unromantic.

OSCAR WILDE

April 13

How a little love and good company improves a woman ...

GEORGE FARAQUHAR

April 14

If two people love each other, there can be no
happy end to it.

ERNEST HEMINGWAY

April 15

Oh, life is a glorious cycle of song,
A medley of extemporanea;
And love is a thing that can never go wrong,
And I am Marie of Romania.

DOROTHY PARKER

April 16

Love is the triumph of imagination over intelligence.

H.L. MENCKEN

April 17

One exists with one's husband — one lives with one's lover.

HONORE DE BALZAC

April 18

Love is a reciprocity of soul and has a different end and
obeys different laws from marriage.

ALESSANDRO PICCOLOMINI

April 19

Every young girl … tries to smother her first love in possessiveness.

GAIL SHEEHY

April 20

Great passions, my dear, don't exist: They are liars' fantasies. What do exist are little loves that may last for a short or a longer while.

ANNA MAGNANI

April 21

He drew a circle that shut me out —
Heretic, rebel, a thing to flout.
But Love and I had the wit to win:
We drew a circle that took him in.

EDWIN MARKHAM

April 22

Love and scandal are the best sweeteners of tea.

HENRY FIELDING

April 23

People in love, it is well known, suffer extreme conceptual delusions; the most common of these being that other people find your condition as thrilling and eye-watering as you do yourselves.

JULIAN BARNES

April 24

To fall in love is to create a religion that has a fallible God.

JORGE LUIS BORGES

April 25

**Terminate torment
Of love unsatisfied
The greater torment
Of love satisfied.**

T.S. ELIOT

April 26

**Give all to love;
Obey thy heart;
Friends, kindred, days,
Estate, good fame,
Plans, credit and the Muse,
Nothing refuse.**

RALPH WALDO EMERSON

April 27

And you must love him, ere to you
He will seem worthy of your love.

WILLIAM WORDSWORTH

April 28

The anger of lovers renews the strength of love.

PUBLILIUS SYRUS

April 29

Love is the drug which makes sexuality palatable in popular mythology.

GERMAINE GREER

April 30

The happiest moment in any affair takes place after the loved one has learned to accommodate the lover and before the maddening personality of either party has emerged like a jagged rock from the receding tides of lust and curiosity.

QUENTIN CRISP

May 1

Shall I compare thee to a summer's day?
Thou art more lovely and more temperate:
Rough winds do shake the darling buds of May
And summer's lease hath all too short a date.

WILLIAM SHAKESPEARE

May 2

Love is fostered by confidence and constancy; he who is able
to give much is able also to love much.

SEXTUS PROPERTIUS

May 3

Aesthetic emotion puts man in a state favorable to the reception of erotic emotion. ... Art is the accomplice of love. Take love away and there is no longer art.

REMY DE GOURMONT

May 4

Love is an irresistible desire to be irresistibly desired.

ROBERT FROST

May 5

No woman ever falls in love with a man unless she has a better opinion of him than he deserves.

ED HOWE

May 6

Love is the wisdom of the fool and the folly of the wise.

SAMUEL JOHNSON

May 7

As soon as you cannot keep anything from a woman, you love her.

PAUL GERALDY

May 8

You don't love a woman for what she says, but love what she says because you love her.

ANDRE MAUROIS

May 9

The course of true love never did run smooth.

WILLIAM SHAKESPEARE

May 10

No man at one time can be wise and love.

ROBERT HERRICK

May 11

Doubt thou the stars are fire,
Doubt that the sun doth move;
Doubt truth to be a liar;
But never doubt I love.

WILLIAM SHAKESPEARE

May 12

Drink to me only with thine eyes,
And I will pledge with mine;
Or leave a kiss but in the cup,
And I'll not look for wine.

BEN JOHNSON

May 13

Courtship consists in a number of quiet attentions, not so pointed as to alarm, nor so vague as not to be understood.

LAURENCE STERNE

May 14

I am not one of those who do not believe in love at first sight, but I believe in taking a second look.

H. VINCENT

May 15

Them must you speak of one that loved not wisely but too well; of one not easily jealous, but being wrong perplex'd in the extreme.

WILLIAM SHAKESPEARE

May 16

Man's love is of man's life a part; it is woman's whole existence.

LORD BYRON

May 17

'Tis better to have loved and lost than never to have loved at all.

ALFRED, LORD TENNYSON

May 18

There are very few people who are not ashamed of having been in love when they no longer love each other.

DUC FRANCOIS DE LA ROCHEFOUCAULD

May 19

It takes a great deal of Christianity to wipe out uncivilized Eastern instincts, such as falling in love at first sight.

RUDYARD KIPLING

May 20

Love is most nearly itself
When here and now cease to matter.

T.S. ELIOT

May 21

Love, which is quickly kindled in the gentle heart, seized this man for the fair form that was taken from me, and the manner still hurts me. Love, which absolves no beloved one from loving, seized me so strongly with his charm that, as thou seest, it does not leave me yet.

DANTE ALIGHIERI

May 22

Love's mysteries in souls do grow,
But yet the body is his book.

JOHN DONNE

May 23

Who then devised the torment?
Love.
Love is the unfamiliar Name
Behind the hands that wove
The intolerable shirt of flame
Which human power cannot remove
We only live, only suspire
Consumed by either fire or fire.

T.S. ELIOT

May 24

Life is eternal; and love is immortal.

ROSSITER WORTHINGTON RAYMOND

May 25

Love at the lips was touch
As sweet as I could bear
And once that seemed too much,
I lived on air.

ROBERT FROST

May 26

Here with a Loaf of Bread beneath the Bough,
A Flask of Wine, a Book of Verse – and Thou
Beside me singing in the Wilderness –
And Wilderness is Paradise enow!

OMAR KHAYYAM

May 27

Of thee I sing, baby,
You have got that certain thing, baby,
Shining star and inspiration
Worthy of a mighty nation,
Of thee I sing!

IRA GERSHWIN

May 28

It is better to love two too many than one too few.

SIR JOHN HARRINGTON

May 29

Men as a rule love with their eyes, but women with their ears.

OSCAR WILDE

May 30

Men have died from time to time, and worms have eaten them – but not for love.

WILLIAM SHAKESPEARE

May 31

The love that lasts the longest is the love that is never returned.

SOMERSET MAUGHAM

June 1

This month is a kiss
Which heaven gives the earth
That she now become a bride
And then a future mother.

ROGER WILLIAMS

June 2

This bud of love, by saucer's ripening breath,
May prove a beauteous flower when next we meet.

WILLIAM SHAKESPEARE

June 3

It is just as hard to live with the person we love as to love
the person we live with.

JEAN ROSTAND

June 4

Gather therefore the Rose, whilst yet is prime
For soon comes age, that will her pride deflower:
Gather the Rose of love, whilst yet is time.

EDMUND SPENSER

June 5

Men make love by braggadocio, and women make love by listening.

H.L. MENCKEN

June 6

Many people when they fall in love can be sure of being admired when they are not admirable, and praised when they are not praiseworthy.

BETRAND RUSSELL

June 7

Love with delight discourses in my mind
Upon my lady's admirable gifts. ...
Beyond the range of human intellect

DANTE ALIGHIERI

June 8

I long to talk with some old lover's ghost,
Who died before the god of love was born.

JOHN DONNE

June 9

Faint heart never won fair lady!
Nothing venture, nothing win —
Blood is thick, but water's thin —
In for a penny, in for a pound —
It's love that makes the world go round

SIR WILLIAM S. GILBERT

June 10

If I love you, what business is it of yours?

JOHANN WOLFGANG VON GOETHE

June 11

A lover without indiscretion is no lover at all.

THOMAS HARDY

June 12

How silver sweet sound lovers' tongues by night,
Like softest music to attending ears!

WILLIAM SHAKESPEARE

June 13

Love bade me welcome: yet my soul drew back,
Guilty of dust and sin,
But quick-eyed love observing me grow slack
From my first entrance in,
Drew nearer to me, sweetly questioning
If I lacked anything.

GEORGE HERBERT

June 14

Love is the emotion that a woman always feels for a poodle,
and sometimes for a man.

GEORGE JEAN NATHAN

June 15

First love is a kind of vaccination that immunizes a man
from catching the disease a second time.

HONORE DE BALZAC

June 16

In order to be happy, one should not know love's passion,
but only love's pleasure.

HELVETIUS

June 17

The realist always falls in love with a girl he has grown up with, the romanticist with a girl from "off somewhere."

ROBERT FROST

June 18

Heav'n has no rage like Love to Hatred turn'd,
Nor Hell a Fury like a woman scorn'd.

WILLIAM CONGREVE

June 19

Love is ... born with the pleasure of looking at each other, it is fed with the necessity of seeing each other, it is concluded with the impossibility of separation!

JOSE MARTI

June 20

O tender yearning, sweet hoping!
The golden time of first love!
The eye sees the open heaven,
The heart is intoxicated with bliss,
O that the beautiful time of young love
Could remain green forever.

FRIEDRICH VON SCHILLER

June 21

Love begets love. This torment is my joy.

THEODORE ROETHKE

June 22

But sometimes a woman's love of being loved
gets the better of her conscience.

THOMAS HARDY

June 23

On wings of song, my dearest,
I will carry you off.

HEINRICH HEINE

June 24

Love has the power of making you believe what you would
normally treat with the deepest suspicion.

HONORE MIRABEAU

June 25

Bid me to live, and I will live
Thy Protestant to be.
Or bid me love, and I will give
A loving heart to thee.

ROBERT HERRICK

June 26

A man may be said to love most truly that woman in whose
company he can feel drowsy in comfort.

GEORGE JEAN NATHAN

June 27

Love is the word used to label the sexual excitement of the young, the habituation of the middle-aged, and the mutual dependence of the old.

JOHN CIARDI

June 28

Oh, when I was in love with you,
Then I was clean and brave,
And miles around the wonder grew
How well I did behave.
And now the fancy passes by,
And nothing will remain,
And miles around they'll say that I
Am quite myself again.

A.E. HOUSEMAN

June 29

It is difficult suddenly to lay aside a long cherished love.

GALUS VALERIUS CATULIUS

June 30

You must remember this, a kiss is still a kiss,
A sigh is just a sigh;
The fundamental things apply,
As time goes by.
It's still the same old story,
A fight for love and glory,
A case of do or die!
The world will always welcome lovers,
As time goes by.

HERMAN HUPFIELD

July 1

Rise up my love, my fair one, and come away.
For, lo, the winter is past, the rain is over and gone;
The flowers appear on the earth; the time of the singing of
birds is come, and the voice of the turtle is heard in our land.

SONG OF SOLOMON

July 2

They that love beyond the world cannot be separated by it.
Death is but crossing the world, as friends do the seas; they
live in one another still.

WILLIAM PENN

July 3

Down by the salley gardens my love and I did meet;
She passed the salley gardens with little snow-white feet.
She bid take love easy, as the leaves grow on the tree;
But I, being young and foolish, with her would not agree.

WILLIAM BUTLER YEATS

July 4

Where love rules, there is no will to power; and where
power predominates, there love is lacking. The one is the
shadow of the other.

CARL GUSTAV JUNG

July 5

Love is either the shrinking remnant of something which was once enormous; or else it is part of something which will grow in the future into something enormous. But in the present it does not satisfy. It gives much less than one expects.

ANTON CHEKHOV

July 6

Cupid: His disgrace is to be called boy, but his glory is to subdue men.

WILLIAM SHAKESPEARE

July 7

As lines so loves oblique, may well
Themselves in every angle greet,
But ours, so truly parallel,
Though infinite, can never meet.

ANDREW MARVELL

July 8

Even memory is not necessary for love. There is a land of
the living and a land of the dead, and the bridge is love; the
only survival, the only meaning.

THORTON WILDER

July 9

Where love is great, the littlest doubts are fear;
Where little fears grow great, great love grows there.

WILLIAM SHAKESPEARE

July 10

Love distills desire upon the eyes,
love brings bewitching grace into the
heart of those he would destroy.
I pray that love may never come to me
with murderous intent,
on rhythms measureless and wild.
Not fire nor stars have stronger bolts
than those of Aphrodite sent
by the hand of Eros, Zeus's child.

EURIPIDES

July 11

Love built on beauty, soon as beauty dies.

JOHN DONNE

July 12

But to see her was to love her,
Love but her – and love forever.
Had we never loved so kindly,
Had we never loved so blindly,
Never met – or never parted –
We had ne'er been broken-hearted.

ROBERT BURNS

July 13

Love in a hut – with water and a crust,
Is – Love, forgive us! – cinders, ashes, dust.

JOHN KEATS

July 14

Absence diminishes mediocre passions and increases great
ones, as the wind blows out candles and fans fire.

FRANCOIS DUC DE LA ROCHEFOUCAULD

July 15

Love is mere madness; and I tell you, deserves a dark house and a whip as madmen do: And the reason why they are not so punished and cured is that the lunacy is so ordinary that the whippers are in love too.

WILLIAM SHAKESPEARE

July 16

The credulity of love is the most fundamental source of authority.

SIGMUND FREUD

July 17

Passion often turns the cleverest men into idiots and makes the greatest blockheads clever.

FRANCOIS DUC DE LA ROCHEFOUCAULD

July 18

When your charms fade,
I shall love thee
When life's dues are paid
I shall love thee
When strom clouds rend the sky
I shall love thee
Forever 'till I die,
I shall love thee

ANONYMOUS

July 19

My merry, merry, merry roundelay
Concludes with Cupid's curse;
They that do change old love for new,
Pray gods, they change for worse.

GEORGE PEELE

July 20

Love, in distinction from friendship, is killed, or rather
extinguished, the moment it is displayed in public.

HANNAH ARENDT

July 21

I loved you, so I drew these tides of men into my hands and wrote my will across the sky in stars.

T.H. LAWRENCE

July 22

What is love? ... It is the morning and the evening star.

SINCLAIR LEWIS

July 23

This is the hardest of all: to close the open hand out of love,
and keep modest as a giver.

FRIEDRICH WILHELM NIETZCHE

July 24

Wine comes in at the mouth,
And love comes in at the eye;
That's all we shall know for truth
Before we grow old and die.

WILLIAM BUTLER YEATS

July 25

Love comforteth like sunshine after the rain.

WILLIAM SHAKESPEARE

July 26

All love is sweet,
Given or returned. Common as light is love,
And its familiar voice wearies not ever …
They who inspire it most are fortunate,
As I am now; but those who feel it most
Are happier still.

PERCY BYSSHE SHELLEY

July 27

Only with those we love do we speak of those we love.

CONRAD RICHTER

July 28

Where love is concerned, it is easier to renounce a feeling
than to give up a habit.

MARCEL PROUST

July 29

Love and a cough cannot be hid.

GEORGE HERBERT

July 30

Language has not the power to speak what love indites:
The soul lies buried in the ink that writes.

JOHN CLARKE

July 31

One word frees us of all the weight and pain of life;
That word is love.

SOPHOCLES

August 1

All love is sweet,
Given or returned. Common as light is love,
And its familiar voice wearies not ever …
They who inspire it most are fortunate
As I am now; but those who feel it most
Are happier still.

PERCY BYSSHE SHELLEY

August 2

Then fly betimes, for only they
Conquer Love that runs away.

THOMAS CAREW

August 3

Who ever loved that loved not at first sight?

CHRISTOPHER MARLOWE

August 4

**My love is of a birth as rare
As 'tis for object strange and high;
It was begotten by despair
Upon impossibility.**

ANDREW MARVELL

August 5

The power of one fair face makes
my love sublime, for it weaned
my heart from low desire.

MICHELANGELO

August 6

"His love is violent but base": a possible sentence. "His love
is deep but base": an impossible one.

SIMONE WEIL

August 7

True love is like seeing ghosts: We all talk about it, but few of us have ever seen one.

FRANCOIS DUC DE LA ROCHEFOUCALD

August 8

Love does not dominate; it cultivates.

JOHANN WOLFGANG VON GOETHE

August 9

Love lessens woman's delicacy and increases man's.

CONRAD RICHTER

August 10

A lover who is absolutely in love does not know whether he
is more or less in love than others, for anyone who knows
this is, just on that account, not absolutely in love.

SOREN KIERKEGAARD

August 11

The speaking in perpetual hyperbole is comely in nothing but in love.

SIR FRANCIS BACON

August 12

Love is a talkative passion.

BISHOP WILSON

August 13

It is as absurd to say that a man can't love one woman all the time as it is to say that a violinist needs several violins to play the same piece of music.

HONORE DE BALZAC

August 14

Love conquers all things; let us too surrender to Love.

PUBLIUS VERGILIUS MARO

August 15

Is it, in Heav'n, a crime to love too well?
To bear too tender, or too firm a heart,
To act a lover's or a Roman's part?
Is there no bright reversion in the sky,
For those who greatly think, or bravely die?

ALEXANDER POPE

August 16

Dear as remembered kisses after death,
And sweet as those by hopeless fancy feigned
On lips that are for others; deep as love,
Deep as first love and wild with all regret;
Death in Life, the days that are no more.

ALFRED, LORD TENNYSON

August 17

No cord or cable can so forcibly draw, or hold so fast, as love can do with a twined thread.

ROBERT BURTON

August 18

Where love is great, the littlest doubts are fear,
When little fears grow great, great love grows there.

WILLIAM SHAKESPEARE

August 19

Ah, when to the heart of man
Was it ever less than a treason
To go with the drift of things,
To yield with grace to reason,
And bow and accept the end
Of a love or a season?

ROBERT FROST

August 20

She that I love is hard to catch and conquer,
Hard, but, O, the glory of the winning were she won!

GEORGE MEREDITH

August 21

Love is not all: It is not meat, nor drink,
Nor slumber, nor a roof against the rain;
Nor yet a floating spar to men that sink.

EDNA ST. VINCENT MILLAY

August 22

Freely we serve
Because we freely love, as in our will
To love or not; in this we stand or fall.

JOHN MILTON

August 23

Perfect love means to love the one through whom one became unhappy.

SOREN KIERKEGAARD

August 24

There are two kinds of faithfulness in love: One is based on forever finding new things to love in the loved one, the other is based on our pride in being faithful.

FRANCOIS DUC DE LA ROCHEFOUCAULD

August 25

The most exclusive love for someone is always a love for something else as well.

MARCEL PROUST

August 26

In love, there is always one who kisses and one who offers the cheek.

FRENCH PROVERB

August 27

Love is the whole history of a woman's life; it is but an episode in a man's.

MADAME DE STAEL

August 28

Lovers' quarrels are the renewal of love.

PUBLIUS TERENTIUS AFER

August 29

To fear love is to fear life, and those who fear life are already three parts dead.

BETRAND RUSSELL

August 30

The maxim for any love affair is: "Play and pray; but on the whole do not pray when you are playing ,and do not play when you are praying." We cannot yet manage such simultaneities.

CHARLES WILLIAMS

August 31

Mourning the loss of someone we love is happiness compared with having to live with someone we hate.

JEAN DE LA BRUYERE

September 1

The magic of first love is our ignorance that it can ever end.

BENJAMIN DISRAELI

September 2

But there is nothing half so sweet in life
As love's young dream.

THOMAS MOORE

September 3

The fickleness of the women I love is only equaled by the infernal constancy of the women who love me.

GEORGE BERNARD SHAW

September 4

Of all man's inborn dispositions, there is none more heroic than the love in him. Everything else accepts defeat and dies, but love will fight no-love every inch of the way.

LAURENS VAN DER POST

September 5

Over the mountains and over the waves,
Under the fountains and under the graves,
Under the floods that are deepest which Neptune obey,
Over rocks that are steepest, Love will find out the way.

ANONYMOUS

September 6

If music be the food of love, play on;
Give me excess of it, that, surfeiting,
The appetite may sicken and so die.

WILLIAM SHAKESPEARE

September 7

To love for the sake of being loved is human, but to love for the sake of loving is angelic.

ALPHONSE DE LAMARTINE

September 8

Love is space and time made directly perceptible to the heart.

MARCEL PROUST

September 9

Love does not consist in gazing at each other, but in looking together in the same direction.

ANTOINE SAINT-EXUPERY

September 10

When poverty comes in the door, love flies out the window.

17TH-CENTURY SAYING

September 11

To be loved, be lovable.

OVID

September 12

Let those love now, who never loved before;
Let those who always loved, now love the more.

THOMAS PARNELL

September 13

I get no kick from champagne,
Mere alcohol doesn't thrill me at all,
So tell me, why should it be true
That I get a kick out of you?

COLE PORTER

September 14

But true love is a durable fire
In the mind ever burning,
Never sick, never old, never dead
From itself never turning.

SIR WALTER RALEGH

September 15

The night has a thousand eyes,
And the day but one;
Yet the light of the bright world dies
Wigh the dying sun
The mind has a thousand eyes,
And the heart but one;
Yet the light of a whole life dies
When love is done

Francis William Bourdillon

September 16

There is no fury like a woman searching for a new lover.

Cyril Connolly

September 17

There is only one happiness in love; to love and be loved.

GEORGE SAND

September 18

The only thing which is not purely mechanical about falling in Love is its beginning. Although all those who fall in love do so in the same way, not all fall in love for the same reason. There is no single quality which is universally loved.

JOSE ORTEGA Y GASSET

September 19

It is a common enough case, that of a man being suddenly captivated by a woman nearly the opposite of his ideal.

GEORGE ELIOT

September 20

Love goes toward love, as schoolboys from their books;
But love from love toward school with heavy looks.

WILLIAM SHAKESPEARE

September 21

The greater the love, the more false to its object,
Not to be born is the best for man;
After the kiss comes the impulse to throttle,
Break the embraces, dance while you can.

W.H. AUDEN

September 22

It's gude to be merry and wise
It's gude to be honest and true;
It's gude to be off with the old love,
Before you are on with the new.

ANONYMOUS

September 23

No woman ever hates a man for being in love with her; but many a woman hates a man for being a friend to her.

ALEXANDER POPE

September 24

The Art of Love: knowing how to combine the temperament of a vampire with the discretion of an anemone.

E. MICHEL CIORAN

September 25

Through all the drama – whether damned or not –
Love gilds the scene, and women guide the plot.

RICHARD BRINSLEY SHERIDAN

September 26

Love me today,
Love me tomorrow,
Love me in joy,
Love me in sorrow.

ANONYMOUS

September 27

**Who does not love wine, women and song
Remains a fool his whole life long?**

JOHANN HEINRICH VOSS

September 28

**Love lodged in a woman's breast
Is but a guest.**

SIR HENRY WOTTON

September 29

Never give all the heart, for love
Will hardly seem worth thinking of
To passionate women if it seem
Certain, and they never dream
That it fades out from kiss to kiss;
For everything that's lovely is
But a brief, dreamy, kind delight.

WILLIAM BUTLER YEATS

September 30

Like love we don't know where or why,
Like love we can't compel or fly,
Like love, we often weep, Like love we seldom keep.

W. H. AUDEN

October 1

Oh heart! oh blood that freezes,
blood that burns!
Earth's returns
For whole centuries of folly, noise and sin!
Shut them in,
With their triumphs and their glories and the rest,
Love is best.

ROBERT BROWNING

October 2

Love, like Death,
Levels all ranks, and lays the shepherd's crook
Beside the scepter.

EDWARD BULWER-LYTTON

145

October 3

True love is fragile
Treat it with care
For it may shatter
And disappear

ANONYMOUS

October 4

Harmony is pure love, for love is complete agreement.

LOPE DE VEGA

October 5

Friendship is constant, in all other things,
Save in the office and affairs of love:
Therefore, all hearts in love use their own tongues;
Let every eye negotiate for itself.
And trust no agent.

WILLIAM SHAKESPEARE

October 6

In peace, Love tunes the shepherd's reed;
In war, he mounts the warrior's steed;
In halls in gay attire is seen,
In harmless dances on the green.
Love rules the court, the camp, the grove,
And men below, and saints above;
For love is heaven, and heaven is love.

SIR WALTER SCOTT

October 7

Romantic love can very well be represented in the moment, but conjugal love cannot, because an ideal husband is not one who is such once in his life, but one who every day is such.

SOREN KIERKEGAARD

October 8

Love is an ideal thing, marriage a real thing; a confusion of the real with the ideal never goes unpunished.

JOHANN WOLFGANG VON GOETHE

October 9

Love between the sexes is a sin in theology, a forbidden intercourse in jurisprudence, a mechanical insult in medicine and a subject philosophy has no time for.

KARL KRAUS

October 10

No disguise can long conceal love where it exists, or long feign it where it is lacking.

FRANCOIS DUC DE LA ROCHEFOUCAULD

October 11

God is Love – I dare say. But what a mischievous
devil Love is!

SAMUEL BUTLER

October 12

The summer hath his joy,
And winter his delights,
Though love and all his pleasures are but toys,
They shorten tedious nights.

THOMAS CAMPION

October 13

All thoughts, all passions, all delights,
Whatever stirs this mortal frame,
All are but ministers of Love,
And feed his sacred flame.

SAMUEL TAYLOR COLERIDGE

October 14

Love is ever rewarded either with the reciprocal, or with an
inward and secret contempt.

SIR FRANCIS BACON

October 15

To rage, to lust, to write, to commend,
All is the purlieu of the god of love.

JOHN DONNE

October 16

Never seek to tell thy love,
Love the never told can be;
For the gentle wind does move
Silently, invisibly.

WILLIAM BLAKE

October 17

If ever thou shalt love,
In the sweet pangs of it remember me;
For such as I am, all true lovers are:
Unstaid and skittish in all motions else
Save in the constant image of the creature
That is beloved.

WILLIAM SHAKESPEARE

October 18

If love were what the rose is,
And I were like the leaf,
Our lives would grow together
In sad or singing weather.

ALGERNON CHARLES SWINBURNE

October 19

If no love is, O God, what fele I so?
And if love is, what thing and which is he?
If love be good from whennes cometh my woo?

GEOFFREY CHAUCER

October 20

If all the world and love were young,
And truth in every shepherd's tongue,
These pretty pleasures might me move
To live with thee, and be thy love.

SIR WALTER RALEGH

October 21

If you love, you will suffer, and if you do not love, you do not know the meaning of a Christian life.

AGATHA CHRISTIE

October 22

Love begins with love; friendship, however warm, cannot change to love, however mild.

JEAN deLa BRUYERE

October 23

It is a mistake to speak of a bad choice in love, since as soon as a choice exists, it can only be bad.

MARCEL PROUST

October 24

Love, kindled by virtue, always kindles another, provided that its flame appears outwardly.

DANTE ALIGHIERI

October 25

Love – is anterior to Life –
Posterior – to Death –
Initial of Creation, and
The Exponent of Earth.

EMILY DICKINSON

October 26

Love, all alike, no season knows
nor clime.
Nor hours, days, months, which are
the rags of time.

JOHN DONNE

October 27

Ah Love! could you and I with Him conspire
To grasp this Sorry Scheme of Things entire?
Would we not shatter it to bits – and then
Remold it nearer to the Heart's Desire?

OMAR KHAYYAM

October 28

A tale without love is like beef without mustard: insipid.

ANATOLE FRANCE

October 29

Let men tremble to win the hand of woman, unless they win along with it the utmost passion of her heart.

NATHANIEL HAWTHORNE

October 30

Familiar acts are beautiful through love.

PERCY BYSSHE SHELLEY

October 31

All's fair in love and war.

Francis E. Smedley

November 1

Love is the state in which man sees things most widely different from what they are. The force of illusion reaches its zenith here, as likewise the sweetening and transfiguring power. When a man is in love he endures more than at other times; he submits to everything.

FRIEDRICH WILHELM NIETZCHE

November 2

O! they love least that let men know their love.

WILLIAM SHAKESPEARE

November 3

I love my love,
My love loves me.
One happy day
We shall be three!

ANONYMOUS

November 4

Love is a boy by poets styled;
Then spare the rod, and spoil the child.

SAMUEL BUTLER

November 5

Love, who is most beautiful among the immortal gods, the melter of limbs, overwhelms in their hearts the intelligence and wise counsel of all gods and me.

HESIOD

November 6

The joy of life is variety; the tenderest love requires to be rekindled by intervals of absence.

SAMUEL JOHNSON

November 7

There was never any yet that wholly could escape love, and never shall there be any, never so long as beauty shall be, never so long as eyes can see.

LONGUS

November 8

The tragedy of love is indifference.

SOMERSET MAUGHAM

November 9

Goodness armed with power is corrupted, and pure love without power is destroyed.

REINHOLD NIEBUHR

November 10

Love yields to business. If you seek a way out of love, be busy; you'll be safe then.

OVID

November 11

No one has ever loved anyone the way everyone
wants to be loved.

MIGNON McLAUGHLIN

November 12

The red rose whispers of passion,
And the white rose breathes of love;
O, the red rose is a falcon,
And the white rose is a dove.

JOHN BOYLE O'REILLY

November 13

Love is a mood – no more – to man,
And love to woman is life or death.

ELLA WHEELER WILCOX

November 14

Love is a sickness full of woes,
All remedies refusing.

SAMUEL DANIEL

November 15

Love is an attempt at penetrating another being, but it can only succeed if the surrender is mutual.

OCTAVIO PAZ

November 16

Then, let thy love be younger than thyself,
Or thy affection can not hold the bent;
For women are as roses, whose fair flower
Being once displayed, doth fail that very hour.

ROBERT BROWNING

November 17

Love is enough, though the world be awaning.

WILLIAM MORRIS

November 18

Love is like measles; we can't have it bad but once, and the
later in life we have it, the tougher it goes with us.

JOSH BILLINGS

November 19

The lover thinks oftener of reaching his mistress than does the husband of guarding this wife; the prisoner thinks oftener of escaping than does the jailer of shutting the door.

HENRI STENDHAL

November 20

The ruling passion, be it what it will,
The ruling passion conquers reason still.

ALEXANDER POPE

November 21

Love begets love. This torment is my joy.

THEODORE ROETHKE

November 22

It is only with the heart that one can see rightly; what is essential is invisible to the eye.

ANTOINE DE SAINT-EXUPERY

November 23

No human creature can give orders to love.

GEORGE SAND

November 24

If music be the food of love, play on,
Give me excess of it, that, surfeiting,
The appetite may sicken, and so die,
That strain again! it had a dying fall:
O! it came o'er my ears like the sweet sound
That breathes upon a bank of violets,
Stealing and giving odor!

WILLIAM SHAKESPEARE

November 25

Love is most nearly itself
When here and now cease to matter.

JOHN MILTON

November 26

In many ways does the full heart reveal
The presence of the love it would conceal.

SAMUEL TAYLOR COLERIDGE

November 27

**Youth's the season made for joys;
Love is then our duty.**

JOHN GAY

November 28

**Jealousy is always born together with love, but it does not
always die when love dies.**

FRANCOIS DUC DE LA ROCHEFOUCAULD

November 29

Love is a spirit all compact of fire,
Not gross to skink, but light, and will aspire.

WILLIAM SHAKESPEARE

November 30

There are two tragedies in life. One is to lose your heart's
desire. The other is to gain it.

GEORGE BERNARD SHAW

December 1

Yet each man kills the thing he loves,
By each let this be heard,
Some do it with a bitter look,
Some with a flattering word.
The coward does it with a kiss,
The brave man with a sword!

OSCAR WILDE

December 2

Everything that man esteems,
Endures a moment or a day,
Love's pleasure drives his love away.
The painter's brush consumes his dreams.

WILLIAM BUTLER YEATS

December 3

It is easier to be a lover than a husband for the simple reason that it is more difficult to be witty every day than to say pretty things from time to time.

HONORE DE BALZAC

December 4

L'amour, l'amour fait tourner le monde. (It's love, it's love that makes the world go round.)

ANONYMOUS FRENCH SONG

December 5

Of all the objects of hatred, a woman once loved
is the most hateful.

MAX BEERBOHM

December 6

Set me as a seal upon thine heart, as a seal upon thine arm:
For love is strong as death; jealousy is cruel as the grave.

SONG OF SOLOMON

December 7

Love to faults is always blind,
Always is to joy inclin'd,
Lawless, wing'd, and unconfin'd.
And breaks all chains from every mind.

WILLIAM BLAKE

December 8

What a woman says to her ardent lover should be written in
wind and running water.

CATULLUS

December 9

Love and War are the same thing, and stratagems and policy
are as allowable in the one as in the other.

MIGUEL DE CERVANTES

December 10

If the heart of a man is depress'd with care,
The mist is dispelled when a woman appears.

JOHN GAY

December 11

So when you or I are made
A fable, song, or fleeting shade,
All love, all liking, all delight
Lies drowned with us in endless night.

ROBERT HERRICK

December 12

The meeting of two personalities is like the contact of two
chemical substances: If there is any reaction,
both are transformed.

CARL GUSTAV JUNG

December 13

Lovers never get tired of each other, because they are always talking about themselves.

FRANCOIS , DUC DE LA ROCHEFOUCAULD

December 14`

A woman without a man cannot meet a man, any man, of any age, without thinking, even if it's for a half second, Perhaps this is the man.

ANONYMOUS

December 15

The heart has its reasons which reason knows nothing of.

BLAISE PASCAL

December 16

To be able to say how much you love is to love but a little.

FRANCISCO PETRARCO

December 17

Love me tender, love me sweet,
Never let me go.

ELVIS PRESLEY / VERA MATSON

December 18

But love is blind and lovers cannot see
The petty follies that they themselves commit.

WILLIAM SHAKESPEARE

December 19

Love means not ever having to say you're sorry.

ERICH SEGAL

December 20

O! how this spring of love resembles an April day.

WILLIAM SHAKESPEARE

December 21

Love is swift, sincere, pious, pleasant, gentle, strong, patient, faithful, prudent, long-suffering, manly and never seeking her own; for wheresoever a man seeketh his own, there he falleth from love.

THOMAS A KEMPIS

December 22

Love lodged in a woman's breast is but a guest.

December 23

**No man has ever lived that had enough
Of children's gratitude or woman's love.**

ANONYMOUS

December 24

The dove loves when it quarrels; the wolf
hates when it flatters.

SAINT AUGUSTINE

December 25

Hatred stirreth up strifes; but love covereth all sins.

PROVERBS 10:12

December 26

There isn't a bourgeois alive who in the ferment of his youth, if only for a day or for a minute, hasn't thought himself capable of boundless passions and noble exploits. The sorriest little woman-chaser has dreamed of Oriental queens; in a corner of every notary's heart lie the moldy remains of a poet.

GUSTAVE FLAUBERT

December 27

Pleasure and love are the pinions of great deeds.

JOHANN WOLFGANG VON GOETHE

December 28

There is a fullness of all things, even of sleep and love.

HOMER

December 29

Love knows nothing of order.

SAINT JEROME

December 30

O, human love! thou spirit given
On Earth, of all we hope in Heaven.

EDGAR ALLAN POE

December 31

**And we are put on earth a little space
That we may learn to fear the beams of love.**

WILLIAM BLAKE